THIS JOURNAL BELONGS TO

Jules Arafa

2/22/23

DATE STARTED   /   DATE COMPLETED

Word First

W O M E N

HOW TO USE THIS JOURNAL

THIS JOURNAL UTILIZES A SIMPLE BIBLE STUDY METHOD TO HELP YOU INTERACT WITH GOD'S WORD EACH DAY. THE INFORMATION BELOW WILL WALK YOU THROUGH HOW TO DIG DEEP INTO SCRIPTURE AND TO REFLECT UPON HOW YOU CAN APPLY IT TO YOUR LIFE. AFTER ALL, IT ISN'T ENOUGH TO JUST READ GOD'S WORD - WE MUST LET IT TRANSFORM US FROM THE INSIDE OUT!

SCRIPTURE

God's Word speaks to every situation or challenge that we will ever face. How comforting to know that we can get our guidance directly from the One who knows and created all things! We can approach His Word with confidence, knowing that every word is flawless and true. Ask God to speak to you through His Scriptures and to reveal His heart to you. We recommend reading the selected Scripture several times before you begin!

OBSERVE

Use this section to record anything that stands out to you or that the Lord has put on your heart. Underline, highlight and write notes on the verse itself. Ask yourself: *What is the verse/passage saying? What stood out and why? What words or concepts do I not understand? (Tip: Look them up!) What did I learn about myself? More importantly, what did I learn about God?* For further context, read the full chapter or passage in your Bible.

TRANSFORM

You've read God's Word. You've analyzed it, researched things you didn't understand and asked yourself important questions about yourself and God. Now, what will you do with that information? Ask yourself: *How can I apply what I just learned to my life today? What practical steps can I take to apply these truths to my life? How will my life change because of this?*

SEEK

End in a time of seeking God in prayer. There is no right or wrong way to pray. Your words don't need to be fancy or eloquent - the Lord knows your heart and longs to communicate with you no matter what. Thank Him for His Word and ask Him to help you store up and apply the things that you have learned **so that you may be transformed!**

SAMPLE

Let the (morning) bring me word of your (unfailing) love, for **I have put my trust in you.** (Show me) the way I should go, for to you I entrust my life.

Psalm 143:8

OBSERVE

Unfailing:
without error or fault
reliable/constant.

He will lead if you ask!

His love will never fail me – why wouldn't I trust Him?

TRANSFORM

Make a habit of meeting with God first thing in the morning! This shows what my priority is and fixes my eyes on Him. There is no better way to start my day!

Trust God's plan over my plan!!!

SEEK

Lord – Thank you for your unfailing love! Forgive me for trying to control my life instead of trusting you, for I know that your plan is always best. Give me the discipline and commitment to meet with you each morning – so that you would be able to guide me each day. Amen.

PREPARE THE WAY

The season of Lent is a time to prepare our hearts for the glorious celebration of Resurrection Sunday. It is a time of remembrance, contemplation and dedication. A time to truly reflect upon the life and death of our Lord, Jesus Christ.

As we follow Jesus to the cross over the next forty days, let us throw off the distractions and doubts that keep us from dedicating our hearts fully to Him. Let us ask ourselves how we can draw near to God and experience His love like never before. This isn't simply about giving something up or starting something new, it's about fixing our eyes on Jesus and letting His sacrifice on the cross transform our hearts and minds - and not just for forty days, but for eternity.

LET US FIX OUR EYES ON JESUS, THE AUTHOR AND PERFECTER OF OUR FAITH, WHO FOR THE JOY SET BEFORE HIM ENDURED THE CROSS. -HEBREWS 12:2

JESUS IS TESTED IN THE WILDERNESS

—

DURING HIS 40-DAY FAST IN
THE DESERT, JESUS CHOSE TO
DEPEND ON HIS FATHER TO
SATISFY HIS DEEPEST HUNGER

Then Jesus was led by the Spirit into the wilderness to be tempted by the devil. After fasting forty days and forty nights, he was hungry. The tempter came to him and said, "If you are the Son of God, tell these stones to become bread." Jesus answered, "It is written: 'Man shall not live on bread alone, but on every word that comes from the mouth of God.'" Then the devil took him to the holy city and had him stand on the highest point of the temple. "If you are the Son of God," he said, "throw yourself down. For it is written: '"He will command his angels concerning you, and they will lift you up in their hands, so that you will not strike your foot against a stone."'" Jesus answered him, "It is also written: 'Do not put the Lord your God to the test.'" Again, the devil took him to a very high mountain and showed him all the kingdoms of the world and their splendor. "All this I will give you," he said, "if you will bow down and worship me." Jesus said to him, "Away from me, Satan! For it is written: 'Worship the Lord your God, and serve him only.'" Then the devil left him, and angels came and attended him.

Matthew 4:1-11

PREPARE

YOUR

HEART

—

TAKE SOME TIME TO PRAYERFULLY

CONSIDER HOW YOU HOPE TO

DEEPEN YOUR DEPENDENCE

ON GOD THIS LENTEN SEASON

LORD, TO YOU I AM SURRENDERING

unkind words
non-essential spending
mindless eating

I AM REPLACING IT WITH

daily devotional, devoted daily
prayer time, prayer as my reaction

WITH THE DESIRE OF

increasing dependence on You

I AM MEDITATING ON THIS VERSE

1 Peter 1:3-9

"HE HIMSELF BORE OUR SINS"

IN HIS BODY ON THE CROSS,

SO THAT WE MIGHT DIE TO SINS

AND LIVE FOR RIGHTEOUSNESS;

"BY HIS WOUNDS YOU HAVE

BEEN HEALED."

——

1 Peter 2:24

DAY 1

I (wait) for <u>the Lord</u>, my soul (waits,)
in His <u>Word</u> I put my hope.

Psalm 130:5

OBSERVE

> all about His timing, His plan is perfect
> not just your body, but your soul must trust in wait
> His Word is alive, our hope is therefore alive
> our hope is eternal & its in Jesus
> waiting = patience
> He is patient w/ us, we should be in return

TRANSFORM

> there is hope in the waiting
> bring every step of the process to Him, He wants to know
> even so, it is well with your soul to rest in the Lord
> if the Word is where my hope lies, it should be my comfort
> putting your hope in the Word is an <u>action</u>
> ⤷ do it daily, that's why it's "daily bread"

SEEK

Lord, thank you for the peace you provide in the waiting.
Let me understand that Your word is Your gift
as a resting place & source of my hope, meant
to be read & reflected upon daily. Allow me
to have the desire to dive into that hope &
equip myself with the sword daily. Amen.

DAY 2

But **He said to me,** "My grace is sufficient for you, for my power is made perfect in weakness. Therefore I will boast all the more gladly of my weaknesses, so that the power of Christ may rest upon me.

2 Corinthians 12:9

OBSERVE

> He says this to me!   Phil 4:13?
> His grace is more than enough
> boast in weakness bc it is opportunity for His power to work
> human weakness is no match for divine power
> therefore! so that! application words!
> gladly!

TRANSFORM

> He entrusts me w my trials
> this is our hope in suffering
> think 1 Peter 1:3 → praise is the response to weakness
> this is all present tense
> weakness is a promise, but so is His power
> this is seeking joy in all

SEEK

Lord, thank you for your heart for us, that in our weakness, you allow for Your power to rest on us. Let this be my focus in hard times, that I have something to boast about because of what is available to me.
Let praise be my response to suffering & trust in the forecast I have in the gospel.
                                        Amen.

DAY 3

I can do all this through Him who gives me strength.

Philippians 4:13

OBSERVE

> this isn't the Lord giving you super powers
> this is about the ability to be content in all things
  ↳ not to reinforce a "triumphalist" mentality
> put in connection with John 15:5
  ↳ we cannot do anything without Him
   – He is giving us strength

TRANSFORM

> suffering is promised, but He is how you get through it
> this strength is the secret
> this is Christ-focused verse, not about us
  ↳ we have to stop making our faith about us
→ IT IS A GIFT.

SEEK

Lord, thank you for your willingness to give us your strength. Thank you for your strength being the tool to help us through any trial & let us also lean on You & Your strength in times of joy as well. Let this be my prayer.
                    Amen.

other translations say "wait"

DAY 4

**But those who hope in the Lord will renew their strength.
They will soar on wings like eagles; they will run and
not grow weary, they will walk and not be faint.**

Isaiah 40:31

waiting on the lord is not passive

OBSERVE

> hope in the lord is the first step
> strength comes from the lord
> He sustains
> renewal!
> He brings it to us when we seek Him
> purpose to move forward & progress for Him

soar = measure
run = purpose
walk = faith

TRANSFORM

1. recognize that (Eph 6) we soar into heavenly places in Jesus
2. set ourselves (Heb 12:1) on the course to win the race
3. then in a good place to walk (Col 2:6) the walk
> "weak" (v.29) & "faint (v.30) are same Hebrew word: failure through loss of inherent strength
> "weary": exhaustion bc of the hardness of life"
   ☆ He gives strength either way! ☆

SEEK

Lord, thank you for such a clear order on where to
get our strength & how those steps allow us
to walk firmly by first recognizing
that it is only because of you. thank
you for renewal & for sustaining us
so our cups overflow! Amen

FOR CHRIST'S LOVE COMPELS US,

BECAUSE WE ARE CONVINCED THAT

ONE DIED FOR ALL, AND THEREFORE

ALL DIED. AND HE DIED FOR ALL,

THAT THOSE WHO LIVE SHOULD NO

LONGER LIVE FOR THEMSELVES BUT

FOR HIM WHO DIED FOR THEM

AND WAS RAISED AGAIN.

———

2 Corinthians 5:14-15

→ deep, serious trouble

DAY 5
"TRIBULATION"

Our responses:

" BE
CONSTANT "

[Be joyful in hope, patient in affliction, faithful in prayer.]
Romans 12:12 ☆ Heb 10:32,36 ☆

↓
"REJOICE"

↳ commanded to do all this w/ an eye towards Heaven

OBSERVE

> hope? it is source of your joy
> affliction? have patience in Him
> consistency in prayer!
  ↳ this verse should be a daily prayer
> hope, affliction, & prayer are guaranteed
> v.13 is all about service, generosity & hospitality

all should come
→ from a heart post
that is established in
this verse

TRANSFORM

> hope is the biggest reason to rejoice & celebrate
> we serve God rejoicing in hope, not in results
> this verse is how we fulfill the command for steadfast character
> "patient": not a passive putting up w things, but active, steadfast endurance
> trials do not excuse a lack of love in the body of Christ or a lack
  of willingness to do this work

SEEK

Lord, let these be my responses! Guide me to become one of
steadfast character, one who does not abandon hope & patience &
prayer. Remind me that patience is an active endurance
& not a passive act of ignorance. Mold me so that this
is my heart posture to serve others & to pursue
You daily!
                    Amen.

DAY 6

But seek first His kingdom and His righteousness,
and all these things will be given to you as well.

Matthew 6:33

OBSERVE

> seeking is ACTIVE
> this is how to order our priorities
> all these things: heavenly treasure, rest in divine provision,
& fulfillment of God's highest purpose for man

fellowship w/ Him & being part of His kingdom!

TRANSFORM

> the choice to seek first is fundamental (made when first repent)
↳ every day after that, our life will either reinforce
that choice or deny it
> this is about heart posture again
> this is always number one on the priorities list
HOW TO START EVERY DAY, THING, TASK, & THOUGHT

SEEK

Lord, let this be my first thought when you bless
me with another day. let my steps & actions be
kingdom led & let my words be bold to share
& sweet like honey w/ your love. let this be
how I order my priorities.
Amen.

DAY 7

it is proud presumption
to take things into our
own worry

**Humble yourselves, therefore, under God's mighty hand,
that He may lift you up in due time. Cast all your
anxiety on Him because He cares for you.**

1 Peter 5:6-7

OBSERVE

> v.5 : "God opposes the proud but gives grace to the humble"
> He knows the due time to exalt us, we are in a humble place @ present
> Matt 6:31-34
> this does not mean our ungodly anxieties
> casting : throw it away from you
> He will lift you up!

TRANSFORM

> casting takes two hands :
   ↳ hand of prayer & hand of faith
> God is not just good, He cares
   ↳ we aren't occupied w/the task of making Him care, of awakening by
        sacrifice or prayer or act the slumbering interest of the Deity
> think yoke & burden

SEEK

lord, let me cast my worries on you & not on others. let me
submit to your plan in humility. Thank you for caring
for me, for not be a slumbering God, but one who
is alive & invested in this creation. let me be reminded
that it is in due time & that your hand is the one
that humbles me & lifts me up.   Amen.

DAY 8

For God gave us a spirit not of fear
but of **power** and **love** and **self-control**.

2 Timothy 1:7

OBSERVE

> our spirits are given to us by God
> we are not made to be fearful
> He made us in His image, so of course we should have second half spirits
> fearful situations that come from fleshly weakness are not from God
   ↳ this is the first step to dealing w these fears
> second step: second half! what He has given us!

TRANSFORM

> power = to do His work, proclaim His word, safe in His hands
> love = Jesus' power is expressed in how much we can love & serve others
   ↳ ☆ John 13:1-11 • washing the feet
> self-control / sound mind = in contrast to the panic & confusion
> we don't need to accept what God hasn't given to us, but walk humbly on what He has
> boldness is how we fill God's purpose

SEEK

Lord, give me boldness to realize fear does not come from you.
that You have given me a second half spirit with which
to fulfill Your purpose for my life & respond with to
fearful situations Let me show others this
spirit & enough to where I get to share the
source where it comes from.
                                    Amen.

WHAT, THEN, SHALL WE

SAY IN RESPONSE TO THESE

THINGS? IF GOD IS FOR US,

WHO CAN BE AGAINST US?

———

Romans 8:31

DAY 9

#Matt 6:6

Rejoice always, pray continually, give thanks in all circumstances;
for this is God's will for you in Christ Jesus.

1 Thessalonians 5:16-18

OBSERVE

- we are to do all three all the time
- pray without ceasing → constant flowing conversation with God
- Jesus is the way to do this! it is the Lord's will!
- the three are intertwined, all exist in harmony
  - ↳ feel out of sync w/o one
- our joy isn't based in circumstance, but in God

TRANSFORM

- "when joy & prayer are married their first born child is gratitude"
- the thought isn't, "this is God's will so you **must** do it"
  - ↳ rather "this is God's will, so you **can** do it"
- it isn't easy, but we can thanks to His will
- we don't give thanks for everything but IN everything
  - ↳ recognize His sovereign hand is in charge

SEEK

Lord, let me live according to your will. that i would
live continuously in all three. rejoice. prayer. thanks. let these
be my first thoughts when i wake & carry them in my
heart as i go through the day. you are so generous &
kind to invite me into such a joyful life as this in
Christ Jesus.
                    Amen.

DAY 10

"...this is the fittest time for connecting w/ God. An hour in the AM is worth 2 in the PM."

→ reference to how you would lay & order your offering

**In the morning, Lord, you hear my voice;
in the morning I lay my requests before you
and wait expectantly.**

Psalm 5:3

↳ upon the altar

OBSERVE

> in the morning = first thing, first response to gift of another day
> lay & wait are both actually action verbs
  ↳ both require conscious decision & daily application
> pray in the morning to honor God at the beginning of the day & set the tone of dedication
> "While the dew is on the grass, let grace drop upon the soul"
> our prayer needs to be directed

TRANSFORM

> "Do we not miss very much of the sweetness & efficacy of prayer
  by a want of careful meditation before it, and of hopeful
  expectation after it? Let holy preparation link hands with
  patient expectation, and we shall have far larger
  answers to our prayers"
  – Charles Spurgeon

SEEK

Lord, let this be my routine. By immediately meeting with you
in prayer when i am gifted another day. give me the
boldness with which to invite you into every part of my life &
my heart & lay it at your feet like an offering.
Give me a spirit of quiet peace in expectancy of your
response.   Amen.

→ *James 1:2*

Blessed is the (one) who **perseveres under trial** because, having stood the test, that person will receive the crown of life that the Lord has promised to those who love Him

ork of God us is evident

James 1:12

OBSERVE

- "stood the test" = shows your dedication & devotion
- starts like a beatitude ☆ Matt 5:1-12 ☆
  ↳ the promise of blessedness is given to the one who endures temptation
→ purpose of God allowing temptation → that through testing we would be revealed as genuine & strong in our faith
- the crown: worth it endure & demonstrate our love for Jesus

TRANSFORM

- "to those who love him": the motive
- the passions of sinful temptations can only really be overcome by greater passions
  ↳ that is a passions for the honor & glory & relationship w/ God
- the best motive for resisting temptation is to love Him
  ↳ to love Him w greater power & greater passion than your love for the sin
- the crown is sure to those who run with patience

SEEK

Lord, let this be a reminder of the motive behind resisting & enduring temptation, that my love for You would be greater than my love for sin. Be with me when trials arise, allow me to feel Your presence & Your lifting hand as temptations arise. You are good & You are kind to reward endurance.
Amen.

DAY 12

asking for nothing
less than a
miracle

**Create in me a pure heart, O God,
and renew a steadfast spirit within me.**

Psalm 51:10

OBSERVE

> not enough to simply clean the heart we already have
> "create" is a plea for a new heart ☆Ezekiel 36:26☆
  ↳ this same Hebrew word is used in Genesis 1
    - only used to describe what only God can do, create out of nothing
> steadfast spirit required to continue in the way of godliness
> humble reliance

TRANSFORM

"A steadfast spirit is needful in order to keep a
cleansed heart clean; and, on the other hand,
when, by cleanness of heart, a man is freed from the
preturbations of rebellious desires & the weakening influences
of sin, his spirit will be steadfast."
                                        - Maclaren

SEEK

Lord, this is my plea, not for a cleansing, but
for a new heart in the new creation that
comes alive in you. You are kind, just, &
THE miracle worker. only you can do
this work in me, oh Lord.
                                        Amen.

14

GREATER LOVE HAS

NO ONE THAN THIS:

TO LAY DOWN ONE'S LIFE

FOR ONE'S FRIENDS.

———

John 15:13

you choose it &
you place it ←

For where your treasure **is, there your** heart **will be** also.

Matthew 6:21

↳ guarantee

can only have your →
treasure in one place:
Heaven or Earth

OBSERVE

> the ancient Greek literally says "do not treasure for yourself
   treasures in earth" (v.19)
> earthly treasure = temporary & fading away
   ↳ not intrinsically bad, but no ultimate value
> heavenly treasure = everlasting & incorruptable
   ↳ give enjoyment now → contentment & sense of well-being that comes
                                        from being a giver

TRANSFORM

" our material treasures will not pass from this life to the
   next; but the good that has been done for the kingdom of
   God through the use of our treasures lasts for eternity, &
   the work God does in us through faithful giving will
      last for eternity. "

SEEK

lord, let this be tucked away in my heart. that no
matter the situation or stage of life, that i am
reminded & brought peace by the fact that my
treasures are heavenly & not on or of the Earth.
thankful & grateful for this to be true!
                              Amen.

DAY 14

dependant

plea/request

Since we live by the Spirit, let us keep in step with the Spirit.

Galatians 5:25

OBSERVE

> stoicheo: ancient Greek for "to walk in line with"
> ↳ to stand beside a person or a thing, hold to, agree with, follow
> the present imperative indicates that this is to be a
    <u>habitual practice</u>
> keeping in step suggests realigning yourself daily
> dependant plea

TRANSFORM

" if the spirit is the source of
your life, let the spirit
also direct its course. "

REVISED ENGLISH BIBLE

SEEK

lord, align my steps daily w the spirit. since you
are the source, be my guide. let my ways
look more & more like yours & less like mine. use
your uplifting hands to correct & adjust me
to walk in line & in truth.
                                        Amen.

DAY 15

And **God is faithful;** He will not let you be tempted
beyond what you can bear. But when you are tempted,
He will also **provide a way out** so that you can endure it.

1 Corinthians 10:13

OBSERVE

> God has promised to supervise all temptation that comes at us through the world, the flesh, or the devil

> He promises to limit it according to our capability to endure it
  ↳ our capability as we rely on Him, not on ourselves

> even as the enemy wanted to destroy Job (1:6-12) & Peter (Luke 22:31), God will not let him

> He provides a way out

TRANSFORM

> He will never force us to use the escape, but He does make it available
  ↳ up to us to take it
  ↳ does not lead us to escape all temptation, but where we might be able to it

> like a mountain pass, the way out isn't necessarily easy

> there is often a wrong way to relieve temptation & we will continue to face it until we show Satan & our flesh we are able to bear it

SEEK

Lord, I know I have fallen into temptation time & time again. It is clear that it is not something that I can defeat on my own, but something I must bring to You every time I face it & not just come to You afterwards when the guilt hits. Let the conviction hit early & my response be prayer.
Amen.

DAY 16

For You created my inmost being; You knit me together in my
mother's womb. I praise You because I am fearfully and wonderfully
made; Your works are wonderful, I know that full well.

Psalm 139:13-14

OBSERVE

> He has the care & concern to personally form each child
> "Knit together" shows the intentionality behind the formation
  ↳ requires precision, time, skill
> David is writing this
  ↳ the science of anatomy was quite unknown to him; &
     yet he had seen enough to arouse admiration & reverence

TRANSFORM

"if we are marvelously wrought upon even before we are born,
what shall we say of the Lord's dealings with us after we
quit his secret workshop, & He directs our pathway through the
pilgrimage of life? what shall we not say of that new birth
which is even more mysterious than the first, & exhibits even
more the love & wisdom of the Lord." - Spurgeon

SEEK

Lord, Your intentionality with which You knit me
together in my mother's womb is unfathomable.
That you not only cared about my physical being
but my inner most soul as well. I am fearfully
& wonderfully made! Let me know that full
well & live that way!
                                   Amen.

I LIFT UP MY EYES

TO THE MOUNTAINS —

WHERE DOES MY HELP COME

FROM? MY HELP COMES FROM

THE LORD, THE MAKER OF

HEAVEN AND EARTH.

———

Psalm 121:1-2

DAY 17

-WILL.

**My flesh and my heart may fail,
but God is the strength of my heart
and my portion forever.**

Psalm 73:26

OBSERVE

> recognize your own weakness
> recognize the strength of God & that enduring character
☆ Numbers 18:20 ☆
↳ in ancient Israel, the priests enjoyed a priveleged status of
having the lord as their "share" & "inheritance"
→ denied privelege of land ownership

TRANSFORM

> "allusion is made here to the division of the promised land. I
   ask no inheritance below; I look for one above"
> God is not only a ~~too~~ heavenly hope
   ↳ He is my earthly desire
   ↳ He is my inheritance in heaven
   ↳ He endures

SEEK

Lord, while it is sure that my flesh will fail
as will my heart, please be my strength
& my portion. that You are my inheritance
& Heaven is where I will recieve that. thank
you for pouring into my cup so consistently
       & intently.   Amen.

appeal to our will

brought alive to the altar
→ stays alive at the altar

Therefore, I urge you, brothers and sisters, in view of God's mercy, to offer your bodies as a living sacrifice, holy and pleasing to God — this is your true and proper worship.

Romans 12:1

"Reasonable service"

OBSERVE

> a plea to the entire body of Christ!
> worship is active!
> foundation of Christian living
> "God calls us to make a choice about the way that we live for Him
> "bodies": entire being
  ↳ He wants us, not just our work

TRANSFORM

> the body is a wonderful servant, but a terrible master
  ↳ must keep it at God's altar
> ☆ 1 Corinthians 6:20
  ↳ God bought our bodies with a price
> "reasonable service" is a life of worship according to God's Word
> worship is an offering!

SEEK

lord, let me be reminded that worship is my offering to You & that it should be my whole self & not shallow. Let my life be a living sacrifice to You!
Amen

DAY 19

→ desire

Then He said to them all, Whoever wants to be my disciple must deny themselves and take up their cross daily and follow me.

& the world

Luke 9:23

→ daily Jesus attitude

↓ self is destined to die

↓ not about self-promotion or self-affirmation

OBSERVE

> invitation is for everyone
> Jesus is telling the disciples this right after He has told them
    that He must get crucified, rejected & suffer
      ↳ calling us to this / have this intention
> carrying a cross always led to death on a cross
      ↳ unrelenting instrument of torture, death, & humiliation

TRANSFORM

> taking up a cross is a one-way journey
> in Roman world, crosses were impressed upon people
      ↳ He is asking us to voluntarily do this
> "this isn't to suggest that we can choose our way to die a living death
    as followers of Jesus; but as the unchosen circumstances come into life, we
    choose to bear them as a way to daily die for Jesus' glory."

SEEK

Lord,

let me have an attitude
like you daily.

Amen.

DAY 20

But just as He who called you is holy, so be holy in all you do; for it is written: "Be holy, because I am holy."

1 Peter 1:15-16

OBSERVE

> holiness = not moral purity but apartness
> God is separate, diff from His creation
  ↳ both in His essential nature
  ↳ & in the perfection of His attributes
> God calls us to come to Him & share His apartness
> holiness is not so much something we possess as something that possesses us

TRANSFORM

> He could have built walls to further separate
  ↳ but He wants us closer
> quoting Leviticus
> wake up & act like you are God's child
> holiness is not a suggestion, it's the standard
> spirit is how we can even strive to be like Him

SEEK

lord,

let me know that this is the family standard.

Amen.

I WILL INSTRUCT YOU AND

TEACH YOU IN THE WAY YOU

SHOULD GO; I WILL COUNSEL YOU

WITH MY LOVING EYE ON YOU.

———

Psalm 32:8

DAY 21

The Lord is my strength and my shield; my heart trusts
in Him, and He helps me. My heart leaps for joy,
and with my song I praise Him.

Psalm 28:7

OBSERVE

> in his trouble, David cried out to God
  ↳ now v.6-7 is him ~~now~~ praising the God who heard & answered
> suddenly the prayer becomes a song of praise
  ↳ an act of adoration
> this is David adding his testimony
> this is great rejoicing

TRANSFORM

"Real praise is established upon sufficient & constraining reasons;
it is not irrational emotion, but rises, like a pure spring, from the
  deeps of experience." - Spurgeon
> David knew that God answered his prayer, perhaps
even before the answer was in hand
> look for the Spirit to bear witness with ours

SEEK

Lord,

when i pray, let me expect
& anticipate an answer, having
confidence instead of hope.
                            Amen.

DAY 22

Do not conform to the pattern of this world, but be transformed by the renewing of your mind. Then you will be able to test and approve what God's will is — His good, pleasing and perfect will.

Romans 12:2

OBSERVE

> world will try to conform us to its ungodly pattern
> battle ground bwn conforming & renewing is the mind
> ✲ Mark 9:2-3; 2 Cor 3:18 ✲
  ↳ transformation takes place as we behold the face of God, spending time in His glory
> your life will be proof
> cannot prove His will w/ your life apart from the Spirit

TRANSFORM

Paul is explaining how to live out His will:
  1. Keep in mind the rich mercy of God to you — past, present, & future
  2. yield your entire self to Him — an act of intelligent worship
  3. Resist conforming to the thoughts & actions of this world
  4. focus on God's word & fellowship w/ Him
     [applicable breakdown of v.1-2]

SEEK

Lord,

let this be my daily checklist
for how to die to self

Amen

27

boldly: <u>NOT</u> proudly, or w/ presumption ←

[BUT]

constantly, w/o reservation, freely, w/ confidence & persistence

"come boldly"

Let us then approach God's throne of grace with confidence, so that we may receive mercy and find grace to help us in our time of need.
Hebrews 4:16

OBSERVE

> an honest plea
> bc He is omnipotent & compassionate, we have access to come boldly to the throne
> mercy & judgement reconciled into one throne of grace
☆REMEMBER: grace does not ignore God's justice, it operates in fulfillment of
       God's judgement, in light of the cross
↘ in light of the finished work of Jesus

TRANSFORM

> He provides help in our time of need
> no request is too small
☆PHIL 4:6☆
  ↳ be anxious for nothing
  ↳ always in prayer
  ↳ make it known to God

SEEK

Lord,

let my heart know & love
Phillipians 4:6!

Amen.

DAY 24

**So whether you eat or drink or whatever you do,
do it all for the glory of God.**

1 Corinthians 10:31

OBSERVE

> live a life focused on glorifying God
> He is the center of all you do
> we must keep this principle in mind
> purpose of our lives: <u>NOT</u> to see how much we can get
away w/ & still be christians
> think how much easier it would've been for the Corinthians!

TRANSFORM

V.32: an offense = an occasion to stumble, leading someone else
into sin, Paul says:
↳ no behavior should encourage that
☆ Galatians 5:11-12 ☆
> low conduct in Christian living is connected to little
regard for the lost

SEEK

Lord,
let me not have low conduct, but
have high reverance for You while
seeking for all to be saved.

Amen.

FOR OUR LIGHT AND

MOMENTARY TROUBLES ARE

ACHIEVING FOR US AN

ETERNAL GLORY THAT FAR

OUTWEIGHS THEM ALL.

———

2 Corinthians 4:17

not to talk about it,
but to do it

Teach me to do your will, for you are my God;
may your good Spirit lead me on level ground.

Psalm 143:10

OBSERVE

> the need to do God's will
> in reliance upon God, you must know God cannot obey for you
> the loving God will teach us
> how we should do the will of God: thoughtfully, immediately, cheerfully, constantly, universally, spiritually, & intensely
> His good spirit connects teaching work of God w presence of His spirit

TRANSFORM

> God guides us by His eye as well as His word
> Holy Spirit speaks in secret whispers to those who are able to hear him
> In light of the outpouring of the Holy Spirit that is part of the New Covenant → we should know that His spirit is good all the more
> a believer has no reason to fail to yield to the presence & power of the Holy Spirit

SEEK

Lord,

Let me yield & accept & lean into Your presence & your spirit.

Amen.

DAY 26

So I say, walk by the Spirit, and you will not gratify the desires of the flesh.

Galatians 5:16

OBSERVE

> simple as that
> it's an either or, cannot both coexist
> Spirit aligns with heavenly things, the desires of flesh are by definition, of this world
> walk by the Spirit instead of trying to live by the law
> does not give license to sin, not pro-legalism

TRANSFORM

> first, Holy Spirit must live in you
> second, must be open & sensitive to this influence
> third, must pattern your life after that influence
> if you walk, you will look like Jesus
> "Life by the Spirit is neither legalism nor license - nor a middle way btwn them. It is a life of faith & love that is above all of these false ways."
(Boice)

SEEK

Lord,

let my life be one by the Spirit & not a middle ground of lukewarm words & actions.

Amen.

DAY 27

Whoever finds their life will <u>lose it</u>,
and whoever loses their life <u>for my sake</u> will <u>find it</u>.
Matthew 10:39

OBSERVE

> open invitation to all ("whoever")
> about sacrifice again
> disciples lived in a paradox
  └ can only find life by losing it, only live by dying
> ressurrection life can only come after:
  └ we take up our cross & follow Him

TRANSFORM

"Bearing the cross, we are to <u>follow after</u> Jesus: to bear
a cross without following Christ is a poor affair. A
Christian who shuns the cross is no Christian; but a
crossbearer who does not follow Jesus equally
        misses the mark."
                                    (Spurgeon)

SEEK

Lord,

let me bear the cross <u>&</u>
  follow You.

                        Amen.

DAY 28

→ put confidence in Jesus

faith in Christ

Jesus said to them, "I am the **bread of life**; **whoever** comes to me shall **not** hunger, and **whoever** believes in me shall **never thirst**."

John 6:35

OBSERVE

> He is hoping to lift up their eyes from material bread & earthly Kingdoms, & on to spiritual realities

☆ 1st "I am" saying of this gospel

> "comes to me" → requires action on our part
  ↳ "receives Him"
  ↳ "not hunger": spiritual hunger satisfied

TRANSFORM

"Coming is a very simple action indeed; it seems to have only two things about it, one is, to come away from something, and the other is, to come to something."

(Spurgeon)

SEEK

Lord,

let me come away & come to.

Amen.

BEING CONFIDENT OF THIS,

THAT HE WHO BEGAN A GOOD

WORK IN YOU WILL CARRY IT

ON TO COMPLETION UNTIL THE

DAY OF CHRIST JESUS.

—

Philippians 1:6

DAY 29

He must increase; I must decrease.

John 3:30

OBSERVE

★ YOU ARE NOT GOD ★
  ↳ sermon by TA (Porch 3/7)
> exalt the God who will be exalted
> humble yourself before you are humbled
★ ISAIAH 2:1-11 ★
> begin to live like you will in heaven

TRANSFORM

> pride = inflated view of self & deflated view of God
> humility = inflated view of God which breeds a deflated view of self
> humility is the key to eternity
> do not be a christian atheist
> think of John the Baptist!
  ↳ may be doing similar ministry, but not the same roll

SEEK

Lord,

let me begin to live like i
will in heaven, preparing everyday
for eternity.

Amen.

DAY 30

At last; final; at the end of it all

might: inherent power or force, reserve of strength

power: exercise of might

Finally, be strong in the Lord and in His mighty power.

Ephesians 6:10

in light of all Paul has written in this book so far there is a battle to fight in the Christian life

OBSERVE

> this is the set-up verse for the armor of God

> think David
  ↳ ☆ 1 Samuel 30:6

> you must be strong in the Lord & THEN put on the armor
  ↳ go through basic training
    > will be given the best weapons & armor, but must be sure you are strong first to make sure you can use what is given

TRANSFORM

> must rely on His might & then do the work
  ↳ by faith, rely on it more & more & . . .

> strength is found in the Lord
  ↳ NOT of ourselves

> we cannot let mindless, busywork of the world sap the strength that we have in Christ, His strength for His work

SEEK

Lord,

let me be strong in you so that i can support Your armor & rely on Your might so that i may do Your work!

Amen.

DAY 31

But because of His great love for us, God, who is rich in mercy, made us alive with Christ even when we were dead in transgressions — it is by grace you have been saved.

Ephesians 2:4-5

OBSERVE

> "But God"!

↳ Paul explained God's reason behind reconciling man to himself

› His rich mercy & His great love

> "for us"!

↳ extends even to children of wrath; we give Him no reason to love us, <u>YET</u>

↳ simply receive while recognizing we are unworthy (grace ~~see~~ secret)

TRANSFORM

✦ John 5:24 ✦

↳ He shared in our death, so we could share in resurrection life

> work of God's grace

↳ no way involving man's merit

↳ our rescue is God's work done for the undeserving

> "dead..." : providing nothing lovable to Him

SEEK

Lord,

let me die to find life in You.

Amen.

March 25
DAY 32

**So do not fear, for I am with you; do not be dismayed,
for I am your God. I will strengthen you and help you;
I will uphold you with my righteous right hand.**

Isaiah 41:10

OBSERVE

TRANSFORM

SEEK

FIXING OUR EYES ON JESUS,

THE PIONEER AND PERFECTER OF

OUR FAITH. FOR THE JOY SET BEFORE

HIM HE ENDURED THE CROSS.

—

Hebrews 12:2

DAY 33

For we do not have a high priest who is unable to empathize with our weaknesses, but we have one who has been tempted in every way, just as we are — yet He did not sin.

Hebrews 4:15

OBSERVE

....

....

....

....

....

....

TRANSFORM

....

....

....

....

....

SEEK

....

....

....

....

....

DAY 34

Because your love is better than life, my lips will glorify you. I will praise you as long as I live, and in your name I will lift up my hands.

Psalm 63:3-4

OBSERVE

....
....
....
....
....
....

TRANSFORM

....
....
....
....
....
....

SEEK

....
....
....
....
....
....

DAY 35

Submit yourselves, then, to God.
Resist the devil, and He will flee from you.

James 4:7

OBSERVE

....
....
....
....
....
....

TRANSFORM

....
....
....
....
....
....

SEEK

....
....
....
....
....
....

DAY 36

What good will it be for someone to gain the whole world, yet forfeit their soul? Or what can anyone give in exchange for their soul?

Matthew 16:26

OBSERVE

....

....

....

....

....

....

TRANSFORM

....

....

....

....

....

....

SEEK

....

....

....

....

....

....

JESUS LOOKED AT THEM AND SAID,

"WITH MAN THIS IS IMPOSSIBLE, BUT

WITH GOD ALL THINGS ARE POSSIBLE.

—

Matthew 19:26

DAY 37

Therefore, with minds that are alert and fully sober,
set your hope on the grace to be brought to you
when Jesus Christ is revealed at His coming.

1 Peter 1:13

OBSERVE

....
....
....
....
....
....

TRANSFORM

....
....
....
....
....
....

SEEK

....
....
....
....
....
....

March 31

DAY 38

The Lord will fight for you; you need only to be still.

Exodus 14:14

OBSERVE

....
....
....
....
....
....
....

TRANSFORM

....
....
....
....
....
....

SEEK

....
....
....
....
....
....

April 1

DAY 39

**I have been crucified with Christ and I no longer live,
but Christ lives in me. The life I now live in the body, I live by
faith in the Son of God, who loved me and gave himself for me.**

Galatians 2:20

OBSERVE

TRANSFORM

SEEK

April 2

DAY 40

Therefore, my dear brothers and sisters, stand firm. Let nothing move you. Always give yourselves fully to the work of the Lord, because you know that your labor in the Lord is not in vain.

1 Corinthians 15:58

OBSERVE

TRANSFORM

SEEK

FOR TO ME,

TO LIVE IS CHRIST

AND TO DIE IS GAIN.

——

Philippians 1:21

REFLECTION

Take some time to reflect on your Lent journey.
Use the following questions to prompt your heart and mind.

1. What was difficult about this journey? What was easy? — Apr 3
2. What did you learn about God? About yourself? — Apr 4
3. How has God worked in your heart the past 40 days? — Apr 5
4. What blessings have come from your Lent journey? — Apr 6
5. How has your perspective changed? — Apr 7
6. How will you let this change the way you live? — Apr 8

SHARE YOUR LENT JOURNEY WITH US!

WORDFIRSTWOMEN@GMAIL.COM

 #WORDFIRSTMOMENTS
@WORDFIRSTWOMEN

Word First

W O M E N

Made in the USA
Coppell, TX
20 February 2023

13144015R00040